Dance

HIP-HOP AND URBAN DANCE

Tamsin Fitzgerald

Heinemann
LIBRARY

www.heinemann.co.uk/library
Visit our website to find out more information about **Heinemann Library** books.

To order:
☎ Phone 44 (0) 1865 888066
 Send a fax to 44 (0) 1865 314091
 Visit the Heinemann Bookshop at www.heinemann.co.uk/library to browse our catalogue and order online.

First published in Great Britain by Heinemann Library, Halley Court, Jordan Hill, Oxford OX2 8EJ, part of Pearson Education.
Heinemann is a registered trademark of Pearson Education Ltd.

Editorial: Sarah Shannon and Robyn Hardyman
Design: Steve Mead and Geoff Ward
Illustration: Sarah Kelly
Picture Research: Maria Joannou
Production: Duncan Gilbert

Originated by Modern Age
Printed and bound by Leo Paper Group

ISBN 978-0431933122
12 11 10 09 08
10 9 8 7 6 5 4 3 2 1

British Library Cataloguing in Publication Data
Fitzgerald, Tamsin
  Hip hop and street dance. - (Dance)
  1. Hip-hop dance - Juvenile literature
  I. Title
  793.3

A full catalogue record for this book is available from the British Library.

Acknowledgements
The publishers would like to thank the following for permission to reproduce photographs:
© Alamy Images pp. **17** (Music Stock), **20** (Philipp Hympendahl), **41** (Andrea Matone); © Bill Mohn p.**39**; © Camera Press p. **35** (Grant Scott); © Corbis pp. **4** (Reuters/Claro Cortes), **5, 29** (Bettmann), **13, 26, 32** (Danser/Nicolas Six), **19** (HSI Productions/ZUMA i); © Getty Images pp. **10** (Frank Micelotta), **18** (Matthew Simmons), **27** (Scott Gries), **30** (Jon Furniss/WireImage), **31** (Dave Hogan), **33** (China Pictures), **40** (Joe Raedle); © PA Photos p. **36** (Empics/Alma Robinson); PYMCA p. **7** (Lenard Smith); © Redferns p. **9** (Paul Bergen); © Rex Features pp. **14–15, 16** (Everett Collection/CSU Archives), **23** (Sipa Pres), **25** (Alex Sudea), **34, 38, 43** (Alastair Muir); © Wayne Simmonds p.**37**.

Cover photograph of break dancing reproduced with permission of © Getty Images/Digital Vision.

Disclaimer
All the Internet addresses (URLs) given in this book were valid at time of going to press. However, due to the dynamic nature of the Internet, some addresses may have changed, or sites may have changed or ceased to exist since publication. While the author and publishers regret any inconvenience this may cause readers, no responsibility for any such changes can be accepted by either the author or the publishers. It is recommended that adults supervise children on the Internet.

CONTENTS

Some words are printed in bold, **like this.** You can find out what they mean by looking in the glossary, on page 46.

STREET CULTURE

We see it in films, on TV in adverts and music shows, and in the theatre. What are we talking about? Hip-hop, or urban dance. Hip-hop dance has not been around for very long, but in the last ten years it has flung itself into our living rooms, on to our cinema screens, into our schools and on to our stages. But what is hip-hop?

Street culture

Hip-hop is a lifestyle. It is based on unique new art forms that developed in the streets out of a need for self-expression. It is commonly thought to contain four elements: **DJ-ing**, **MC-ing**, **graffiti** and **b-boying** (break dancing).

How did hip-hop begin? Who are the past and future pioneers of this exciting dance style? How do you go about learning this style, and what place does it have in the future of the theatre? For the history we need to turn to the United States and look at the music, the art, the people and, of course, the streets.

▶ B-boys hit their moves on the streets as crowds gaze on in amazement.

4

An era of change

During the 1960s the United States experienced great social and economic changes. It was a time of great unrest, including protests against the Vietnam War, and young Americans began to question the power of the government and of big corporations. This atmosphere helped the growing civil rights movement, which demanded full rights for black Americans.

The social unrest of the 1960s was expressed in popular music by musicians such as the Beatles, Jimi Hendrix and Bob Dylan. The dance world was going through a time of experimentation, rejecting trained dancers, traditional sets and costumes for a more basic look and feel. Social dances such as the Twist, Mashed Potato and Locomotion took hold of the teenage population.

The birth of hip-hop

In the **Bronx** district of New York city poverty was rife, gangs were everywhere and crime was on the increase. Young people were looking for a means of self-expression and a way to create a sense of identity. They began to experiment with music, dance, art and speech. Out of this experimentation, out of the Bronx, grew a new wave of sub-culture – hip-hop.

Biography

Earl Tucker
Some of the origins of hip-hop dance are credited to a dancer called Earl Tucker, known as 'snake hips'. Tucker performed in **Harlem** music clubs in the 1920s and early 1930s and his moves are considered similar to some early break dance moves.

▼ These protestors are demonstrating against the Vietnam War in the US capital, Washington D.C., in 1969.

FOUR ELEMENTS OF HIP-HOP

Out of the unrest in America, the self-expression and experimentation of the young, came the four elements of hip-hop: **b-boying** (break dancing), **DJ-ing**, **MC-ing** (rapping), **graffiti**. These four elements paved the way for a wave of amazing new artists who catapulted hip-hop culture across the globe. The artists turned b-boying into what we know today as one of the main urban dance styles.

Dance Facts

Hip-hop culture

KRS-One, a legend in the hip-hop world who formed Boogie Down Productions and has released classics such as 'Criminal Minded', believes there are nine elements to hip-hop. These are the original four plus **beatboxing**, hip-hop fashion, hip-hop slang, **street knowledge** and **street entrepreneurship**.

B-boying

B-boying or breaking is the dancing, or physical expression, of hip-hop. B-boying began on the streets with little more than a 'boom box' (a large portable sound system) and a piece of cardboard to spin on. B-boying is about a lifestyle that involves dedication and passion. It is about style, dancing, battling, power and families. It began with James Brown, Afrika Bambaata, and the Rock Steady Crew and is now one of the fastest-growing and most evolving styles of dance.

DJ-ing

DJ-ing is the musical expression of hip-hop. It involves using turntables, records, mixers and **scratching**. The first person to use these techniques was DJ Kool Herc. He used twin turntables to cut back and forth between tracks, and extended the instrumental sections (which dancers would dance to), to create a new sound known as the '**break**'. It was called this because there was a break from the **lyrics**. DJ-ing is now a massive industry. DJs are sometimes called '**turntabilists**'. They scratch, mix records and compete to win titles in the same way as those involved in the other elements of hip-hop.

Graffiti artists demonstrate their skill on the New York subway carriages.

MC-ing

MC-ing, or rapping as it became known, is the verbal expression of hip-hop. It involves speaking to the beat of the music using rhyme. It may relate to a theme or send out an important message. Kool Herc and the Herculoids were the first to MC, and since then MC-ing has developed into a huge industry. Competitions take place all over the world.

Graffiti

Graffiti is the visual expression of hip-hop. It began in the 1960s when a well-known graffiti artist, Taki 183, regularly marked the New York subway with his tag (identification). Soon, many young people were 'graffing' whole sides of trains with messages, names and art. This is depicted in the film *Style Wars* (1983). It is important to know that graffiti activity is illegal. If caught, graffiti artists can face arrest for vandalism (destroying or defacing public property). Famous graffiti artists such as Banksy in the UK have won awards for their work, but their faces remain secret so that they are not arrested.

B-BOYING AND CREWS

When we think of **b-boying**, or break dancing, we think of **head spins**, **windmills**, the **worm**, **freezes** and general displays of gravity-defying movement. B-boying hasn't always been this way.

In the late 1960s in New York, poverty was rife, fighting and gangs were commonplace, and there were 'turf wars' (fights to claim territory) between rivals. The Black Spades were one of the biggest and toughest gangs in New York at the time. The young in the **Bronx** district were looking for a voice and a way to prove they had a future.

The godfather of soul

At this time, the performer James Brown, who was known as 'the godfather of soul', was gaining popularity. His dancing style involved fast and **raw** movements such as spins, quick shuffles, knee drops and the splits. A craze soon followed called the 'Good Foot', named after his hit 'Get on the Good Foot'. This was later renamed 'The B-Boy'. It involved high energy-based dance moves and it formed a framework for b-boying.

Biography

B-boys of the 1970s
The first wave of b-boys included the Zulu Kings, Klark Kent, the Amazing Bobo and Jon Sizzle. The second wave included Jimmy J, Phase 2 and Melle Mel. The third wave include Ken Swift, Frosty Freeze and Crazy Legs.

The godfather of hip-hop

Some young people and gangs in the Bronx started b-boying. B-boys in different gangs started battling with their moves instead of their weapons. This form of battle was called **up rock** and it involved no physical contact. Up rock gave way to other dance moves such as **down rock** or **floor rock**. This was b-boying in its earliest form, with none of the power moves we see today.

In 1969, hip-hop musician Afrika Bambaataa founded Zulu Nation, an 'international hip-hop awareness group'. As b-boying emerged, he decided that it could lead to something positive for a lot of gang members, and he encouraged young people to keep dancing. He set up one of the first b-boy **crews**, the Zulu Kings. The Zulu Kings was made up of local Bronx kids who would perform at talent shows and in clubs. They quickly gained respect and popularity.

▼ Respected hip-hop legend Afrika Bambaataa spins his tunes.

This first wave of b-boy popularity lasted until 1977. Afrika Bambaataa encouraged change, and gave hope to many. He saw that gang violence was reduced as a result of the rise of hip-hop.

Crews

A **crew** is a group of individual b-boys or b-girls who have come together. They see themselves as a family. Each crew has a unique style but one common purpose – to be the best. They do this by competing and being crowned champions. A crew can have many members, but it normally competes using between six and ten members.

▲ These original members of The Rock Steady Crew demonstrate their moves at the VH1 hip-hop honours in the US in 2004.

The Rock Steady Crew

In 1977, two **Bronx** b-boys, Jimmy D and Jojo, established a crew called The Rock Steady Crew. To get into The Rock Steady Crew you had to be the best b-boy, battling to win your place. However, by this stage, the craze of **b-boying** had died down and the Freak, another dance style, was the new fad.

It was not until 1981 that things began really to take off for The Rock Steady Crew. The photographer and sculptor Henry Chalfant offered the crew a chance to perform at the Lincoln Center, Outdoors Program, in Manhattan. The performance was also a battle with rival b-boys from The Dynamic Rockers. It was covered by local television stations, as well as by publications including the *New York Times*, the *Village Voice*, the *Daily News* and *National Geographic*. The performance was a turning point in hip-hop history, as it took the style to a much wider audience. Jimmy D took notice of the craze that had started in Manhattan. He made three influential members of the crew – Crazy Legs, Frosty Freeze and Ken Swift – into President and Co-Vice Presidents of The Rock Steady Crew.

The Rock Steady Crew performed at the Ritz nightclub alongside a punk rock group called Bow Wow Wow, Afrika Bambaataa and the Jazzy 5. After their performance, Crazy Legs and Frosty Freeze asked Afrika Bambaataa if they could be part of the Zulu Kings, the most highly respected of all b-boy crews. Afrika Bambaataa allowed not only them but also the entire Rock Steady Crew to become members of the Zulu Kings. He knew that they would play an important role in spreading the peaceful message of Zulu Nation.

Amazing Fact

Royal invitation
The Rock Steady Crew had major success performing all over the world. In 1983, they were asked by the Queen to perform at the Royal Variety Performance in London. During this time, Charisma Records approached the crew with a record deal. Their record 'Hey You, The Rock Steady Crew' reached number 38 in the US charts. It did much better in the United Kingdom, soaring to the top 10 and selling over 1 million copies.

Breaking

In the 1980s, the media started to call b-boys and b-girls 'breakers' or 'break dancers'. The phrase 'break dance' is now widely used to describe the dancing, but it is not considered to be a true hip-hop phrase and dancers working within hip-hop would still describe themselves as b-boys or b-girls.

Breaking boundaries

B-boying has developed in many ways over the years. With b-boys pushing their bodies to extremes, breaking is now even more daring. As b-boys work to add an extra spin, **flare** or hop to outdo their competitors, the boundaries are constantly being broken.

Head spins involve b-boys spinning on their heads using their legs to control or increase the number of spins. From some of the basic **freezes**, such as a shoulder freeze, b-boys have searched for smaller body parts to balance on. Innovations include balancing on two hands to the forearm, one hand, elbow and even the knuckles, and being upside down, sideways, inverted or turning.

Dance Facts

Korea's relationship with b-boys

B-boying in South Korea has grown into a massive cultural phenomenon. In 2002, Korean b-boy crew Expression won the Battle of the Year title in Germany. They were followed in 2004 and 2005 by Korean crews Gambler and Last for One. This winning streak gave the crews international respect and recognition, and the city government of Seoul, its tourism board and commercial sponsors, started to fund Korean B-boys. B-boys in Korea are used to promote the city and its culture, in the same way that pop or film stars are in the United Kingdom and United States. The capital, Seoul, even has its own b-boy theatre, where b-boy shows are performed all year round.

▼ French Crew Pokemon, winners of many a b-boy battle, perform their crew routine.

Across the globe

Breaking is a worldwide phenomenon, with **crews** and soloists from across the globe competing to be crowned champions. The French crews Vagabond and Pokemon are two of the best. Vagabond were the Battle of the Year Champions in 2006 and Pokemon won the World Crew Title at the 2006 UK B-Boy Championships. Other crews to watch out for are the Korean crews Extreme and Expression as well as the UK crew Soul Mavericks and Mortal Combat from Japan.

Biography

Tip Crew

Tip Crew from Korea won the crew element of the Sony Ericsson B-Boy Championships in 2007. Korea produces some of the world's most extreme dancers, with the most daring moves.

B-GIRLS FIGHT BACK

B-girls have the same history as b-boys, but it has taken longer for the girls to establish themselves in the world of hip-hop. B-girls have often found themselves on the edge of a b-boy **crew.** Due to the power and strength needed for some of the breaking moves, in the past b-girls often found themselves sidelined, left to do footwork and some basic **freezes.**

▼ B-girls strut their stuff at the 3rd annual World Hip-Hop Championships in the US, in 2004.

Today, though, b-girls are fighting back and firmly establishing themselves within the b-boy scene. With their own crews, competitions and festivals, b-girls have now firmly found their place in the male-dominated world of hip-hop and have been given the respect they deserve.

Best b-girls

The UK's first b-girl was Hanifa Macqueen-Hudson, formally known as 'Bubbles'. She rose to fame in the 1980s. Asia One from the United States has long been known not only as one of the best b-girls but also as a businesswoman, because she promotes hip-hop on a global scale. As the creator of the annual B-Boy Summit, an international four-day conference for b-boys and b-girls, Asia One has gained respect and recognition for her work worldwide. Other top b-girls and crews making their mark on a global scale are Rokafella from the **Bronx** (USA), Firefly (UK), Dirty Mamas (Germany), Shebang Crew (Canada), Female Artistics (Austria), Da Ladie Breakers (Hong Kong) and No Easy Props (USA).

Dance Facts

b-boy and b-girl words
'bite' – steal a move
'sick' – really good
'wack' – not very good
'heavy' – amazing
'props' – respect

FUNK STYLES

Funk styles form a collection of street dance styles that come under the umbrella of hip-hop dance.

Locking

Locking is a style of street dance that features strong arm and hand movements with cool, relaxed hips. Wrist rolls, bounces, pauses and points make up some of the movements, along with a cheeky performance style. It is funky, fast and full of synchronized moves that were originally performed to funk music.

In 1969 in Los Angeles, California, a street dancer named Don Campbell was doing a new dance style which he called the 'Campbellock'. He formed his own company of dancers called the Lockers. The Lockers had a very distinctive style. They wore bright colourful shirts, striped socks, cropped trousers, bow ties, white gloves, platform shoes and hats. The Lockers would move using both choreographed routines and through **improvizing**. For the improvized sections, they would stand in a line with some taking

▶ The hit US TV show *The Soul Train* started in 1970. It featured R&B, soul and hip-hop artists, helping to make the latest fashions and dance trends popular.

turns to step forward, make up moves on the spot and then step back. As the Lockers became more famous they made appearances on the hit US TV programme *Soul Train*. This helped to make locking more popular.

The robot

At around the same time locking was developing, another new style of funk dance was beginning to make waves among dancers. The hit TV show *Lost in Space*, inspired dancers like Charles Washington 'Robot' to do a dance called the robot. The robot is a style of movement where the dancer imitates a robot by contracting and releasing their muscles to make the robot move. The robot dance caught on quite quickly, but was later popularized even more by Michael Jackson in his moonwalk. The moonwalk gives the illusion that the dancer is walking forwards, while he is actually moving backwards.

Boogaloo

In Fresno, California, a dancer called Sam Solomon (Boogaloo Sam) was inspired by both Charles Washington and the Lockers. He invented a new style called Boogaloo, named after James Brown's song 'Do the Boogaloo'. Boogaloo took its influences from both the robot and locking. Boogaloo uses every part of the body and includes rolling the hips, knees and head.

In 1977, Boogaloo Sam formed a group called The Electronic Boogaloo Lockers. Later they were renamed The Electric Boogaloos. The Electric Boogaloos are still dancing today, teaching and keeping the 'funk' alive.

Technique

Popping
Popping involves contracting and relaxing muscles to create a popping effect, normally known as a hit or pop. Some other funk styles include floating, strobing, tutting, puppet, scarecrow, waving and ticking.

▲ The originators of funk, The Electric Boogaloos, perform on stage at Breaking Convention in Birmingham, 2007.

NEW DEVELOPMENTS

With **breaking**, **locking**, **popping** and other street dance styles firmly established in hip-hop culture, it was inevitable that new moves and styles would appear on the scene. As hip-hop dance continues to develop and evolve, other influences are finding their way into this world. The term 'urban dance' is now commonly used to describe these.

Clowning and krumping

In 1992, Tommy the Clown entered the arena and a new style of urban dance and clowning was created. Clowning involved dancing at children's birthday parties, dressed as a clown, doing a mixture of street dance moves. Tommy realized that he could offer young people an alternative to gangs, drugs and violence through creativity and expression. He created a following of hip-hop clowns. In his Academy the word 'krump' was used to describe the intensity of a dance move, and **krumping** was born. Since then clowning has grown into a global phenomenon, with performances worldwide.

In 2005, a film documentary *Rize* was created by award-winning director and photographer David LaChapelle. *Rize* introduced the world to a new form of hip-hop dance which involved the use of brightly coloured costumes and make up.

▶ Tommy the Clown performs to the camera at the Rock this Way Tour in Hollywood 2005.

▲ These dancers from the film *Rize* are demonstrating their krumping moves.

Spiritual warfare

Krumping is different to clowning. It does not involve wearing make-up or a costume and is highly energetic. It is sometimes called spiritual warfare. It involves movements such as chest pops (the thrusting of the chest in and out), stomps and arm swings. Krumping is a progression of clowning and is growing in popularity all the time.

As well as the new waves of clowning and krumping there are also other forms of urban dance appearing in studios across the globe. Some of these include house, funk, street jazz, new wave hip-hop and street flava.

Technique

Krump moves

'flashy' – quick foot movements and sharp, precise, showy moves

'goofy' – the least aggressive of the krump styles, usually funny and energetic (pioneered by the krump practitioner Goofy)

'jerk' – motions that are not smooth and flowing but still artistic

'rugged' – fewer tricks; more of a pure essence

'technical' – mix of flashy and smooth; a crowd-pleasing style

Parkour

Parkour or free running was created by a French performer called David Belle. It is a way of travelling across obstacles to reach a destination. Belle describes it as 'like being chased across an urban landscape and having to get over obstacles in the most efficent way possible'. It is daring, graceful and athletic, and it contains movements from diverse disciplines such as gymnastics, climbing, martial arts and acrobatics.

Parkour is becoming increasingly popular. In the same way that the world became aware of break dance, parkour is finding its way into commercials, pop videos, films and onto the stage. Like **b-boying** it has begun to make its way from the streets into theatres. It has been seen in the UK's Royal Variety Performance and is used within the hip-hop theatre Kompany Malakhi's latest show *Boxin*.

▼ A young parkour crew fly through the air, demonstrating the danger and beauty of this recent urban art form.

It is the athletic combination of bird-like movement, heart-stopping acrobatics, spins and jumps, mixed with vertigo-inducing fear that makes parkour so exhilarating. In a recent production called *Traces* by a French-Canadian circus/dance troupe called 7 Fingers, elements of parkour could be seen as an acrobat jumped and flew between two poles.

New combined with old

Other influences that have found their way into the world of urban dance are from other urban art and sport forms such as basketball, skateboarding, tap and circus skills. Yet, like basic ballet technique, b-boying has some fundamental steps that remain untouched and pure. A six-step (where your feet move in six steps around your hands) will always be a six-step, even if the style in which it is performed by the b-boy or b-girl varies.

Urban dance is not alone when it comes to using other influences. Ballet and contemporary dance have long borrowed styles from each other, and influences from hip-hop are now making their way into modern dance.

Step 1

Step 2

Step 3

Step 4

Step 5

Step 6

◀ This movement is the Six Step, an essential movement for anyone learning hip-hop.

HIP-HOP DANCE AND MUSIC

Hip-hop dance and music have always gone hand in hand. It was the innovation of the music that inspired the dance style of **b-boying**. The two follow each other closely, and the music that is played while b-boys and b-girls break is very important. It can set the pace, dynamics, move and style of the dance. The tracks chosen by the **DJs**, the way the music is mixed and the break in the music and the **lyrics** can all determine whether or not the track becomes popular. There are many artists today who have echoes of hip-hop in their music, such as Justin Timberlake and Rihanna, but they are not hip-hop artists in the true sense of the word. For many, hip-hop is a way of life and not something that can be added to sell a record.

The 1960s and 1970s

As we have seen, hip-hop music originated in the **Bronx** in the late 1960s and early 1970s. At parties, DJs would separate the percussion sections between the verses in songs to create an extended 'break' in the music. DJ Kool Herc is one of the originators of hip-hop music. Using funk, soul and disco music, Herc started using an audio mixer and two records. This allowed him to mix two records together. Not long after this, Grand Wizard Theodore invented **scratching**, the art of moving the record back and forth under the needle in a rhythmic fashion.

At these parties, people would keep the party-goers entertained in between songs. They would introduce the tunes, hype the crowds and entertain. They became known as MCs ('MC' stands for 'Master of Ceremonies'). The first MC crew was Kool Herc and the Herculoids. From **MC-ing** came rap. MCs began rhyming what they were saying, **improvizing** on the spot. Rappers, on the other hand, learned their lyrics beforehand and generally would rap about their lives, themselves or important social or political topics. Some of the first rap records were Grandmaster Flash's

'Super Rappin' and the Sugarhill Gang's 'Rapper's Delight'. This type of hip-hop became known as East Coast hip-hop because it originated in New York, on the east coast of the United States.

The 1980s

By the 1980s hip-hop was really popular. New artists such as LL Cool J, Kurtis Blow and Run DMC released records that hit the mainstream charts. Collaborating with the rock artists Aerosmith, hip-hop artists Run DMC had global success with 'Walk this Way'. Female hip-hop duo Salt-N-Pepa also arrived on the scene in 1985. They were the first black female group to have success with tracks such as 'The Show Stoppa' and 'Push It'.

▲ Female hip-hop duo Salt N Peppa in 1984, rapping and dancing their way to worldwide success.

West Coast hip-hop

West Coast hip-hop exploded onto the scene in the late 1980s, with artists such as Dr Dre, Ice T, Snoop Doggy Dog and Tupac Shakur. It is more commonly known as gangsta rap. This type of hip-hop was more melodic but the lyrics were often controversial, creating an image that brought publicity but also problems. The abusive content of the lyrics was perceived by some as promoting violence, racism, sexism and **homophobia**. Some gangsta rappers disagree with this, saying that the lyrics just represent the struggles of their inner-city lives.

Electro

Another style of music to come out of the early hip-hop scene was electro (or electro funk). Body **poppers** often choose to dance to electro. This is because it contains electronic sounds, has a strong beat with a natural pop or hit, and the vocals are sometimes robotic and distorted electronically. Afrika Bambaataa's 'Planet Rock' was one of the first electro records. It was followed by Hashim's 'Al-Naafiysh' (The Soul).

Dance Facts

Turntablist competitions
When turntablists compete, they each perform a routine – a combination of various technical scratches, beat juggles (changing a sample) and other elements including body tricks (using various body parts such as the elbow, chin, back and even nose to mix and scratch records). Invisibl Skratch Piklz is one of the best turntablist crews. It consists of American and Filipino DJs.

Other musical influences

Hip-hop music, like hip-hop dance, has always used outside influences. Be it rock, metal or house, it is constantly changing and progressing. Hip-hop is now a huge global business, with new artists creating new sounds all over the world. Artists, the music they produce and the dance performed to this music in videos and on TV shows influence what we perceive to be popular or fashionable. A lot of the time the dance styles we are seeing relate more to jazz dance than to hip-hop dance.

In the same way that **b-boying** has a competitive nature so does hip-hop music, with competitions in **MC-ing**, rapping, **turntablism** and **beatboxing**.

Dance Facts

Human beatbox

The term 'beatbox' was used as slang for drum machines produced in the late 1970s that could not be programmed. When people could not afford to buy these, they used their mouths instead to create the beats. In the 1980s there were three pioneers of this art form: Darren 'Buffy' Robinson, Doug E. Fresh and Biz Markie. In the late 1990s, artists such as Killa Kela and Rahzel pushed beatboxing to new levels. They added new music styles such as **drum 'n' bass**, and introduced vocal **scratching** and singing and beating at the same time.

▲ Beat boxer Killa Kela drops some beats at a performance at the Scala, London, in 2007.

HIP-HOP AND CLOTHING

When we think of hip-hop or urban dance we think of baseball caps, baggy trousers, oversized t-shirts, bandannas and, of course, the all-important trainers. Hip-hop dancers tend to wear baggy clothes that are comfortable to dance in. This is less true of commercial hip-hop, however. On TV shows and in hip-hop videos, women often wear very little clothing, typically bikini tops and hot pants.

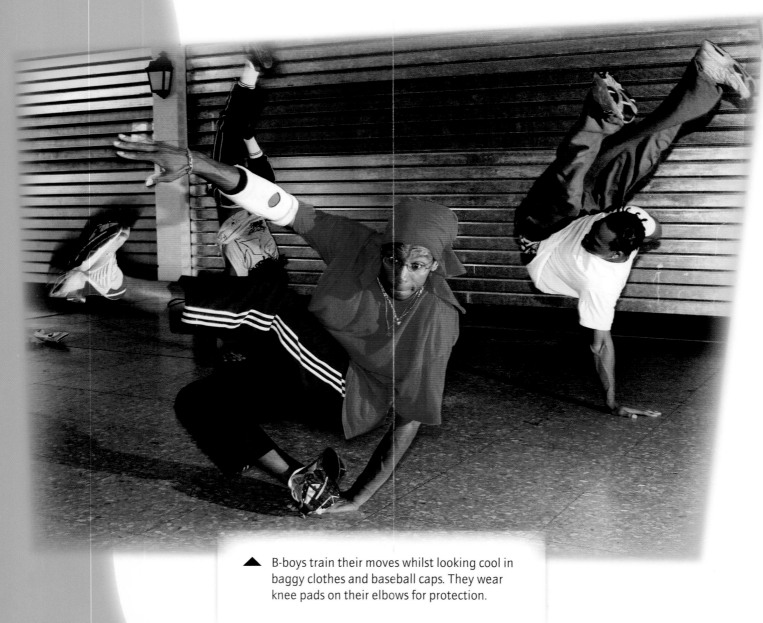

▲ B-boys train their moves whilst looking cool in baggy clothes and baseball caps. They wear knee pads on their elbows for protection.

Essential hip-hop fashions

Image and hip-hop run side by side, and the clothing worn often makes a statement about the person who is dancing. There are few official rules on the clothing, but there are several essential items:

- baseball cap – used by **b-boys** to protect their heads when **head spinning** and often used as a prop in routines
- knee pads – worn by urban dancers under their trousers to protect their knees and also sometimes to protect their elbows
- bandanna – often seen hanging out of a dancer's back pocket, wrapped around the wrist or the head
- trainers – the make, colour and style are all-important.

▲ Hip-hop artist Missy Elliott has developed her own clothing label with a famous sportswear brand.

Promoting brands

In the 1980s fashion and hip-hop combined, as many sports brands used hip-hop artists to promote their clothing and footwear. Hip-hop artists Run DMC were often seen wearing the infamous striped tracksuits of a famous sports brand. In recent years, other hip-hop artists have developed their own clothing labels including Sean 'P. Diddy' Combs and Jay-Z's Roca Wear. Mr Simmons, who launched Def Jam Records, also launched the successful clothing brand Phat Farm in 1993.

Other hip-hop artists, such as female rap icon Missy Elliott, have also been used to promote brands of sportswear. More recently, b-boys and b-girls have been advertising hair products and cars.

URBAN DANCE IN COMMERCE

Urban dance can now be seen in music videos, films and even in computer games. Over the last five years its popularity has grown massively, due to the stars who are dancing it and the products that are made to sell it.

Music videos

In music videos, dance movement is set to a music track by the artist or choreographer. Some pop artists dance in their own videos, others hire dancers to star alongside them. One of the most respected artists and dancers is the US star Michael Jackson.

Michael Jackson is thought by many to be one of the most natural, stunning and inspirational dancers of all time. He has helped to popularize dance styles such as the moonwalk. In his 1983 video 'Thriller', Jackson and his dancers perform a variety of street dance styles that show **popping** and **locking** influences. The dancing in the video is slick, exciting and involves intricate routines. 'Thriller' was the most influential pop video of its time. It rewrote the rules and opened up endless possibilities for the music video.

More recently, a range of music stars including Usher, Missy Elliott and the Black Eyed Peas have used elements of different street dance styles in their music videos.

Amazing Fact

'Thriller'
Michael Jackson's 'Thriller' video was 14 minutes long. It contained body popping and street dance styles. At the time it was the most expensive music video ever made, costing about $US 1 million. The 'Thriller' album sold more than 50 million copies worldwide – more than any other album before it.

Films

In the last five years many films have been made that revolve around urban dance and hip-hop culture. One of the first films to take on this subject was *Style Wars*, which was made back in 1983. *Style Wars* was a documentary focusing on the emerging hip-hop scene in New York. Other dance documentary films followed.

A recent break dance documentary is *Planet B-Boy* (2007), which looks at b-boys today. It follows five **crews** leading up to and taking part in the Battle of the Year competition in Germany.

Computer games

In 2006 *B-Boy*, the first ever computerized b-boy game, was launched. You can battle, pick characters and try dance combos at a series of different events. It also features some classic funk and hip-hop tracks to dance to.

◀ Michael Jackson performs his moves on stage in 1984. Jackson made the moonwalk famous and inspired many dancers with his sensational routines.

HIP-HOP AND CHOREOGRAPHY

When hip-hop dance is performed, it can be both **choreographed** and **improvized**. This is different to most other styles of dance, which are normally entirely choreographed. There are many different areas where choreography is used. These include pop videos, **b-boy** competitions, hip-hop theatre and when hip-hop is mixed with other dance forms.

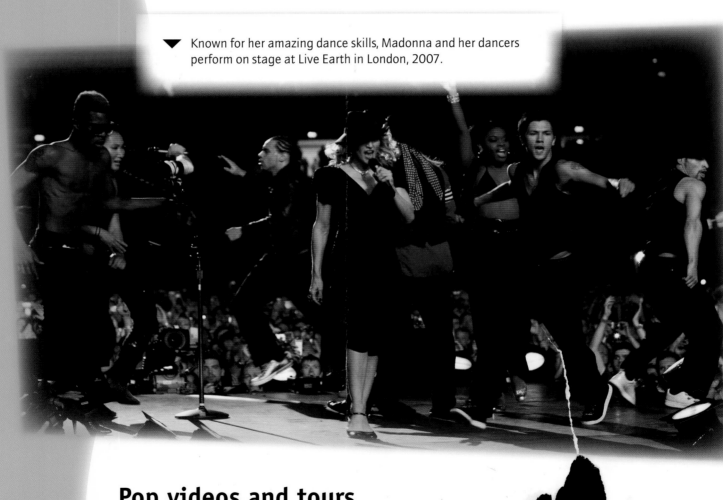

▼ Known for her amazing dance skills, Madonna and her dancers perform on stage at Live Earth in London, 2007.

Pop videos and tours

As a recording artist, there is a huge am
pop video gains mass appreciation o
hottest choreographer to create t
stunning visuals has become es

Jamie King

In the last ten years, there has been one major force behind some of the most unique and explosive pop videos and tours. Jamie King is now recognized as one of the most innovative directors and choreographers working in the music industry today. Born in Verona, Wisconsin, King studied dance at the West Side Performing Arts Studio in Madison, Wisconsin, before gaining a scholarship to the Tremaine/Sleight Dance Studio in Los Angeles. In 1993 King worked for the popstar Prince, who taught him about the fusion of music and movement, as well as staging and lighting. In 1995 King won an Emmy Award Nomination for his work on the American Music Awards. He then worked for Salt-N-Pepa, En Vogue, Michael Jackson, Smashing Pumpkins, Britney Spears, Ricky Martin and many others, before building a long partnership with Madonna.

King worked alongside Madonna from 1996 to 2006 to create the ideas for her videos and world tour. For this he picked up an MTV Award Nomination and was catapulted into the spotlight. King uses urban dance styles in his choreography. He takes the story of the music as a starting point, then creates his routines. For Madonna's world tour she was accompanied by a **crew** of top break dancers.

In 2005, King linked up with a famous sportswear brand to produce a workout DVD and fitness programme which is now taught in gyms across the world. Using a variety of hip-hop moves, cardio, stretching and other dance styles the workout is a fusion of sport and dance.

Biography

Marty Kudelka

Marty Kudelka is an American choreographer to the stars. Originally a b-boy, Marty soon became a teacher, setting up his own studios in Dallas. He crafted his skills there before moving to LA and establishing himself as a leading choreographer. Kudelka co-choreographed Janet Jackson's world tour 'All For You' and worked with Pink and NSYNC. He went on to choreograph Justin Timberlake's pop videos 'Like I Love You', 'Cry Me A River', 'Rock Your Body' and 'Señorita', which helped launch Timberlake's career as a solo artist.

▲ Pop star and stunning dancer Justin Timberlake holds a 'freeze' as he performs on his UK Tour in 2003.

B-BOY COMPETITIONS

The ultimate goal for any young budding b-boy or b-girl is either to be crowned world champion or to win the world **crew** title. **B-boying** has always been about competing with your opponents for the best style and moves. Earning a place to compete in the world championships takes hours of practice and dedication. To be the ultimate winner requires an extra-special touch. Hundreds of competitions take place across the globe. Battles between solo b-boys or b-girls, crews, **lockers** and **poppers** can take many forms.

The circle

In the early days, b-boys would start to dance and onlookers would gather round in a circle. When they finished their moves other b-boys watching would come in to the circle and challenge them. Battles were born. The circle has remained an essential part of b-boying, and battles take place all over the world.

▼ Korean b-boys perform at the Battle of the Year in 2004. Known for their insane power moves, fluidity and dynamic precision, Korean b-boys are the world b-boy champions.

▲ These Chinese b-boys are midway through a head spin.

Battles

Battles between b-boys or b-girls and crew battles are sometimes judged by the crowd watching, and sometimes by a panel of experts. Different battles have different rules, but generally b-boys are judged on style, **top rock**, footwork, **freezes** and power. Other factors are innovation (new ideas), knowledge and execution (how you carry out a move or series of moves).

Crew battles are normally made up of up to eight b-boys or b-girls from a crew. The battles often involve aspects of **choreographed** routines using partner work, acrobatics, power and combinations. These can be judged on synchronicity (performing moves exactly together), difficulty, stage presence (projecting confidence) and use of music. B-boys and b-girls always choreograph their own material for a battle, as the moves and routines they produce represent their crew and style.

From flexibility and strength to agility and acrobatics, b-boying can only be described as daring, explosive, athletic, skilled and powerful. With b-boys trying to outdo each other by discovering the next new move or by adding just one more spin, the art of b-boying will constantly develop.

HIP-HOP THEATRE

Hip-hop theatre uses the traditional elements of theatre, such as performing on a stage, using lighting, sets and costumes, but it also adds the four elements of hip-hop: **DJ-ing**, **MC-ing**, **graffiti** and **b-boying**. Most performances will involve a theme or narrative, sometimes surrounding a character involved in hip-hop. When a dance company performs hip-hop theatre they are normally known as a hip-hop dance theatre company.

Rennie Harris

The main name in US hip-hop theatre is Rennie Harris, a highly acclaimed **choreographer**. Growing up in Philadelphia, Harris was heavily involved in the early hip-hop scene, dancing with Step Masters, the Scanner Boys and Magnificent Force. He has taught workshops at many world-class universities and dance centres including UCLA (University of California in Los Angeles), Columbia College and the Broadway Dance Centre in New York.

▼ Dancers from Rennie Harris's production of *Students of the Asphalt Jungle* perform their footwork moves.

Harris formed the company Pure Movement and has created many pieces of hip-hop theatre including *Lorenzo's Oil*, *Facing Mekka* and *Rome & Jewels*, which premiered in 2000. *Rome & Jewels* uses b-boying, **popping**, **locking** and other street dance forms in a dramatic and athletic re-telling of the classic Shakespeare tale *Romeo and Juliet*. It is the longest-touring hip-hop dance theatre work in US history, and it continues to impress audiences around the world today.

Dance Facts

Awards for 'Rome & Jewels'
Rome & Jewels has received five awards: three Bessie Awards and two Black Theatre Alvin Ailey Awards. It has also received nominations for a Herb Alpert Award and a Lawrence Olivier Award (UK).

Jonzi D

In the United Kingdom, Jonzi D is a leading figure in hip-hop dance theatre, at the cutting edge of current developments. He learned to dance in the 1980s and his influences were The Rock Steady Crew, Poppin Pete and Poppin Tacho from *Breakdance, The Movie*. He trained at the London School of Contemporary Dance and in 1995 created Lyrikal Fearta. When Jonzi first started creating his work he felt that he was the only person doing this style. 'To me it completely made sense to use break dance and popping as a way of finding new movement.'

▶ Jonzi D is the UK's pioneer of hip-hop theatre, and the director of Breakin Convention.

Jonzi D has worked with many dance companies, in the UK and abroad, including Benji Reid (see box), Robert Hylton and ACE Dance and Music. He works with other dance styles as well as hip-hop. He says that when he creates work he starts from a theme, usually taken from the **lyrics**. 'I don't choreograph. I devise and direct. I then bring in choreographers that suit the overall theme. I am a ChoreoPoet.'

He has helped to create fashion shows including *40 degrees* (2006) at Earls Court and *State Property* for Rocawear at the Royal Festival Hall. Jonzi is also an MC and a poet, and he has worked with many artists including Mannafest and Gangstarr. Currently he runs Jonzi D Productions, which is an Associate Company of Sadler's Wells Theatre in London.

▼ Dancers performing Jonzi D's latest work, *TAG…Me vs. The City*. The show explores the idea of using the body to create words (physical calligraphy).

Jonzi D believes that hip-hop theatre is about creating dramatic performances using the styles, techniques and values that come from hip-hop culture. 'It is important to remember the roots of hip-hop and that this dance style grew out of a group of kids expressing themselves, going to clubs and battling.'

Today his influences are Frank II Louise (France), Project Soul (Korea) and Kennrick (UK) from urban dance outfit Boy Blue.

Biography

Benji Reid

Benji Reid's influences when growing up were Jeffy Daniels, Michael Jackson and Raymond Campbell. In 1986 he was the European Body Popping Champion and he came second in the World Dance Championships. He trained at the Northern School of Contemporary Dance in Leeds. He has made a name for himself as a dancer, actor, creative producer, deviser and director. In 1996 he co-directed *Aeroplane Man* with Jonzi D and later toured *Paper Jackets*. He has since produced and directed many shows including his latest work, *Life of a B-Boy*. This piece of hip-hop theatre uses break dance, text and live DJ-ing. Benji now runs the Breaking Cycles theatre group, which is a national and international voice for hip-hop theatre. It plays a key role in the development of hip-hop theatre as an art form.

HIP-HOP AND THE DANCE WORLD

Hip-hop has influenced many different areas of the dance world today.

Contemporary dance

With contemporary dance companies striving to be the most innovative, to work with the hippest choreographers and to sell tickets to an ever-changing audience, contemporary dance has had to make changes. With hip-hop dance attracting big audiences, contemporary dance has found a new competitor. Changing its image into one that is hip, fashionable and cutting edge is something that can be seen both on and off stage.

Rambert, a UK-based contemporary dance company, has a new fashionable website with stunning images that show the changing face of the company. Hip-hop moves including freezes, footwork and acrobatics can clearly be seen, mixed in with more balletic and contemporary styles. In the pieces *Infinity* by Australian choreographer Garry Stewart and *Anatomica #3* by Canadian choreographer André Gingras, we see influences from gymnastics, yoga, break dance and even what seems to be a giant skateboard ramp, from which dancers jump, dive and fall.

Influenced by hip-hop dance, the Rambert Dance company performs Australian choreographer Garry Stewart's *Infinity* 2007.

Victor Auijada's ballet *Suspension of disbelief* combines traditional ballet with hip-hop moves.

Another major contemporary dance company, based in the UK, is Bonachela Dance. Choreographer Rafael Bonachela has created works influenced by hip-hop and pop. He choreographed Kylie Minogue's *Show Girls* tour. His work bridges the gap between urban and contemporary dance.

Modern ballet

In modern ballets we also see the influence of hip-hop. As traditional ballet companies have produced more modern ballet, and modern ballet companies renamed themselves contemporary dance companies, it was not going to be long before the worlds of hip-hop and ballet merged.

The Pacific Northwest Ballet from the United States is a traditional ballet company producing classics such as *Swan Lake*, *The Nutcracker* and *Giselle*, yet they are also producing modern ballets. In 2006 they engaged the choreographer Victor Quijada to create a new work for them. A former b-boy and dancer with Twyla Tharp Dance, Quijada created a work called *Suspension of Disbelief*, which is a unique mixture of break dance and ballet. For him the two styles work well together, as the refined is mixed with the **raw**. *Suspension of Disbelief* won critical acclaim.

The partnership between hip-hop dance and choreography is developing all the time. From the explosive routines in the b-boy competition to the slick, synchronized pop video, from **devised** hip-hop theatre to the fusion of the classical and urban styles, hip-hop dance is still being explored.

TRAINING FOR URBAN DANCE

There are many opportunities for the urban dancer these days, either in the commercial world or in the theatre. Urban dancers can dance in pop videos, perform with a dance company or enter **b-boy** competitions.

▲ These students in a hip-hop class are learning an uprock, one of the basics of break dance.

Formal training

Formal dance training is studying dance at a practical level in preparation for a career in dance. This normally takes place at a dance school, college or conservatoire and you can enter at the age of 16 or 18.

Many dance schools offer courses that cover some elements of urban dance such as **locking**, house dance or street jazz. The training is very competititive, so to get a place at one of these schools you generally need to have previous dance experience and a flair for performnce.

From the street

As urban dance styles flood onto our TV screens, more and more young people are learning the latest moves direct from movies or pop videos. Some of the best urban dancers working today have taught themselves, rather than been trained in a traditional way. This is not always easy. You have to be very motivated. You can decide to attend regular classes at a local dance centre. This is always a good idea as you may get to work with fantastic teachers, as well as find new inspiration.

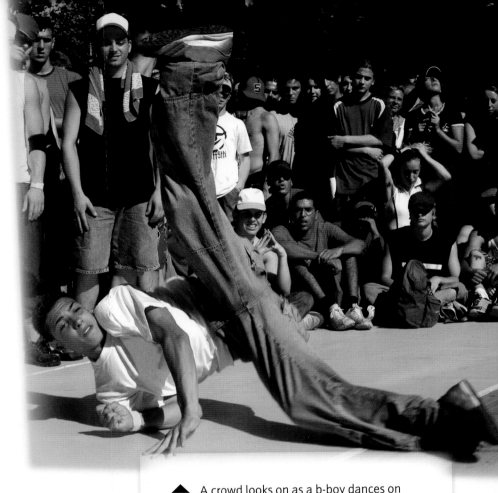

▲ A crowd looks on as a b-boy dances on the streets. This b-boy is halfway through a power move called a windmill.

If you want to become a b-boy or b-girl and enter competitions, training is a very different story. Although dance centres may offer break dance classes, some b-boys would say learning in this way goes against the origins of the dance style. The style and individuality of the moves are best learned in an informal setting.

Some hip-hop theatre and dance companies are looking for dancers with a wide range of skills, who can b-boy as well as do ballet or contemporary dance. Formal dance training may then be necessary.

How to train

The type of training you choose is a personal decision and can depend on what career you would like in the future – dancer, **choreographer**, teacher or b-boy/b-girl. It is always important to get advice if you are not sure.

NEW DIRECTIONS FOR HIP-HOP

In 2004, Jonzi D brought hip-hop to the masses with the United Kingdom's first ever festival of hip-hop, called Breakin Convention. It has continued every year since. With companies from the UK (Boy Blue), US (Electric Boogaloos) and Europe (Frank II Louise) performing, the dance world stood up and began to take notice. Theatrical displays from some of the world's legendary hip-hop artists, as well as from emerging talent, took hip-hop to a new level.

In 2006, Benji Reid's Breaking Cycles ran Process 06, two weeks of discovery and development for the next generation of **hip-hop headz** led by some of the leading hip-hop practitioners in dance, theatre and music.

Hip-hop is everywhere today. Leading artists and companies working in the field of hip-hop dance in the United Kingdom and United States are Jonzi D, Benji Reid, Funk Stylerz, Robert Hylton and his company Urban Classicism, Freshmess, 2FaCeD DaNcE Company and Mickael Marso Riverie's Company Decalage. Also in the US you can see hip-hop influences in the work of dance companies Alvin Ailey, Hubbard Street Dance, Bill Shannon and Bill T. Jones & Arnie Zane Dance Company.

Urban dance shows now regularly go on tour. With conferences for b-boys, break dance moves in dance exams and the influence of hip-hop in other art forms, what paths will hip-hop dance now take? In the future hip-

Dance Facts

Hip-hop awards
Breakin Convention's 2007 UK Tour was nominated by the Theatrical Management Association for Achievement in Dance for exposing the energy and appeal of hip-hop dance theatre to audiences across the UK. Jonzi D was also named a MOBO (Music Of Black Origin) Top 10 Hip Hop **Role Model**. Bill T. Jones and Arnie Zane Dance Company and their collaborators have recently won a Bessie Award for exceptional achievements in **choreography**, for their performance of *Chapel/Chapter* at **Harlem** Stage.

hop or urban dance will surely involve new fusions with other creative forms. As it picks up pace and gains a reputation for being exciting and explosive, what we can certainly say is that hip-hop is on the move.

'The future is acknowledging global and regional development in hip-hop dance. The best new ideas have always come from the street in music and dance. The effect this has had on the dance world throughout history is obvious. Once jazz dance was a street form. Now it is a staple of musical theatre and taught in theatre schools. The future of hip-hop is therefore inevitable.'

Jonzi D

▼ US dance theatre company Alvin Ailey performs *Firebird* at Sadler's Wells, London in 2007.

TIMELINE

Hip-hop dance is currently one of the world's biggest-growing dance genres and industries. Here is a summary of its short history.

1925 'Snake Hips' Earl Tucker performs moves that later inspires **b-boying**.

1960s – small beginnings
The civil rights movement emerges in the United States. The unrest felt in society is mirrored culturally. Out of the **Bronx** comes a new sub-culture: hip-hop.

1966 Political **graffiti** begins to appear across cities in the US, gaining the attention of the press and public.

1969 Afrika Bambaattaa forms Universal Zulu Nation.

1969 First wave of b-boys.
Don Campbell invents the funk dance style **locking**.

1970s – b-boying finds its feet
The world of b-boying takes off.

1971 *New York Times* publishes an article on graffiti artist Taki 183.

1972 TV programme *Soul Train* starts, featuring the Lockers.
James Brown releases 'Get on the Good Foot'.

1974 Universal Zulu Nation is re-named Zulu Nation.
Second wave of b-boys.

1977 Third wave of b-boys.
The Rock Steady Crew is formed.
Electric Boogaloo Lockers is formed.

1979 Sugarhill Gang release the single 'Rapper's Delight'.

1980s – break dance and the media
B-boying becomes break dance, the media discovers hip-hop, and rap develops its first female stars.

1981 The Dynamic Rockers and The Rock Steady Crew battle at the Lincoln Center, New York.

1982 The Rock Steady Crew perform at the Ritz nightclub, New York.

1983 The Rock Steady Crew release the single 'Hey You, The Rock Steady Crew'.
The documentary *Style Wars*, exploring New York's graffiti scene, is first shown on TV.

Rapper Ice T releases his first single.

The Rock Steady Crew make a guest appearance in the film *Flashdance* and on the Royal Variety Performance in the UK.

Run DMC release the iconic single 'It's Like That'.

Michael Jackson first performs the moonwalk on Motown 25 TV special and his 'Thriller' video is released.

The Fat Boys (Darren 'Buffy' Robinson, Doug E Fresh and Biz Markie) win a talent competition at Radio City Hall, New York, sparking the first wave of **beatboxers**.

1985 Female rappers Salt-N-Pepa burst onto the music scene.

1986 Benji Reid becomes European body popping champion.

1990s – clowning, krumping, beat boxing and clothing
Hip-hop finds new areas of influence

1990 The first annual b-boy battle, International Breakdance Cup, is launched.

1991 Mr Wiggles from Electric Boogaloos and some members of The Rock Steady Crew produce the first hip-hop musical, *So What Happens Now?*

1992 Tommy the Clown makes his mark on the hip-hop scene by introducing it to **krumping**.

1993 Clothing label Phat Farm is formed.

1994 The first B-Boy Summit is held in San Diego, California.

1995 Jonzi D creates Lyrikal Fearta.

1996 Benji Reid and Jonzi D direct the film *Aeroplane Man*.

1999 Rahzel (also known as 'The Noise') releases one of the most influential beatboxing albums of all time.

2000s – a new era for hip-hop dance
Hip-hop dance theatre storms onto our stages, Korea battle their way to the top of the b-boy league and b-boying takes on its history with conferences and workshops.

2000 Rennie Harris premieres *Rome & Jewels* with his company Pure Movement.

2001 Korea explodes onto the b-boy scene.

2002 The film *The Freshest Kids – History of a B-Boy* is released.
Crazy Legs of The Rock Steady Crew is inducted into the Hip-Hop Hall of Fame.

2004 The first festival dedicated to hip-hop dance, Breakin Convention, takes place at Sadlers Wells, in London.

2005 The documentary film *Rize* is created by director David La Chapelle and later released.
US director/choreographer Jamie King releases a hip-hop workout video.

2006 Skeeter Rabbit, a former member of the Electric Boogaloos, dies.
The first b-boy computer game is released.
Suspension of Disbelief, created by Victor Quijada, wins critical acclaim.
Benji Reid's theatre group Breaking Cycles runs 'Process 06' for emerging **hip-hop headz**.

2007 The documentary film *Planet B-Boy* is released.
The Rock Steady Crew's 30th anniversary.

GLOSSARY

b-boying (also called 'break dancing') athletic, stylized and fast-paced form of dance where dancers (b-boys or b-girls) often perform and compete

beatboxing (also called 'vocal percussion') art of producing drum sounds, musical sounds, singing or scratching by using the mouth, lips, tongue, voice and teeth

break instrumental or percussion section in a track of music

Bronx borough (region) of New York on the mainland, often considered to be the home of hip-hop

choreography art of making dances

crew group of b-boys or b-girls

devise when a group of artists work together to develop an original theatre or dance production. It is different to choreographing as it involves more than one person's ideas.

DJ-ing (short for 'disc jockey') someone who plays records to entertain people in clubs or on the radio

down rock rhythmic weaving of legs and feet in a continuous circle low around the hand that carries the dancer's weight

drum 'n' bass type of electronic dance music in which the beat is normally between 160–180 beats per minute

flare (also known as a gym flare) break dance move where the dancer supports themselves with their hands and rotates their legs around their body

floor rock old-style break dancing that took place entirely on the floor, involving fast paced and complex footwork

freeze break dance move where the dancer is completely still, or frozen, normally balancing on a body part, such as the hands, elbow or head and shoulders

fresh looking good

graffiti art of spraying, painting or drawing images or names

Harlem neighbourhood in New York City, with a high percentage of black residents

head spin spinning headstand. A b-boy will often use his legs to either control or increase the number of spins.

hip-hop headz slang term for a person who is totally dedicated to hip-hop

homophobia fear of and prejudice against homosexuals

improvise make something up on the spot

krumping energetic form of street dance involving large upper body movements

locking style of street dance that features strong arm and hand movements with cool relaxed hips

lyrics words that are set to music

MC-ing when a person speaks, freestyles or performs to an audience to keep a party or performance going. MC is short for Master of Ceremonies.

popping funk and street style of dance where the dancer contracts and releases their muscles

raw untrained and natural

role model someone that young people look up to and model themselves on

scratching art of moving a record back and forth under the needle in a rhythmic fashion. It used in turntablism and also copied in beatboxing (vocal scratching).

street entrepreneurship to create something out of nothing. People who organize or promote a business from the streets.

street knowledge news and issues of a community passed on from one generation to the next through talking

top rock upright movements performed at the beginning of a break dance set

turntablism musical art form that involves changing the sounds produced by records using turntables and a mixer

up rock dancing 'battle', in which the dancers are very close but do not actually touch

windmill core of most power moves, a back spin and hand glide freeze combined

worm move done either forwards or backwards by shifting the weight from the upper body to the lower body, creating a rippling motion

FURTHER INFORMATION

Books

Soreen Baker, *The History of Rap and Hip-Hop* (Lucent Books) 2006
Louise Chipley Slavicek, *Hip-Hop Stars: Run DMC* (Chelsea House Books) 2007
Peter Shapiro, *The Rough Guide to Hip-Hop*, (Rough Guides) 2005

Websites

If you want to discover more about hip-hop dance check out these websites.

www.yde.org.uk
Youth Dance England will give you a list of organizations that run dance classes in your local area as well as advice and guidance on things dance-related.

www.ukbboy.info
The UK's b-boy community. It contains news, moves, information on b-boy competitions and a great forum for chatting to other b-boys worldwide.

www.bboyworld.com
The website for all things b-boy. See also bboy tube from this website. Features breaking and beatboxing videos.

www.cdet.org.uk
This website will guide you through courses that offer full-time training in dance in the UK. It can also answer questions on funding, qualifications and application.

www.pineapple.uk.com
Based in London, Pineapple dance offers classes in over 40 different styles including locking, popping, hip-hop and break dance, as well as master classes from top professionals.

www.urbanfreeflow.com
The website for all things related to parkour and free running.

INDEX